Finding God
in the Mess

Meditations for Mindful Living

Jim Deeds & Brendan McManus, SJ

LOYOLA PRESS.
A JESUIT MINISTRY

3441 N. Ashland Avenue
Chicago, Illinois 60657
(800) 621-1008
www.loyolapress.com

All photographs by Brendan McManus, SJ (except the following images)
*If there is more than one picture on a page the pictures are listed
top to bottom, left to right.*
v Eliks/Shutterstock.com. **1** Roobcio/Shutterstock.com.
5 primopiano/Shutterstock.com; Arti_Zav/Shutterstock.com;
RaZZeRs/Shutterstock.com; EllenM/Shutterstock.com.
53 PeopleImages/E+/Getty Images. **110** Lizavetta/Shutterstock.com.

Designed by Messenger Publications Design Department

ISBN: 978-0-8294-4910-5
Library of Congress Control Number: 2019943306

Printed in the United States of America
19 20 21 22 23 24 25 26 27 28 Versa 10 9 8 7 6 5 4 3 2 1

Contents

Preface

Jim and Brendan both live in Belfast, Ireland and have sought peace and meaning in what is a beautiful but also fractured and broken city. Keeping oneself engaged and committed, while at the same time reflective and centered, is a difficult balance.

Life is too precious to waste, and the authors have some unique insights about how to live more fully and in tune with reality. Modern lives can be busy and saturated by technology and media, but these don't often bring happiness. As this book proves, it is the time out, the ability to look back and understand life events, that brings about deeper, more satisfying living. Paradoxically, it is looking back and understanding your lived experience that allows you to live with more vibrancy in the present, even if it is messy.

Life is difficult but not impossible, and can be rich and fulfilling. Difficult situations of conflict, stress, and worry arise, as do pleasant situations, but there are ways through these challenges. It is essential to believe that there is something positive in everything, that God is in it somewhere, and that we can get through it with help. Often the problem is that we tend to catastrophize or think the worst of others and of ourselves, and it doesn't help us to deal with the issues. The other problem can be holding on too tightly to our identity or security and blaming everybody else, God, and the world for our problems. Developing awareness and psychological distance helps us realize that bad things can happen to everybody, as good things do. Crucially, it is not about us personally, and there is always a way forward with some divine inspiration.

People often create a false division between their lives, chaotic and challenging, and things spiritual, spotless and holy. Many feel they have to be good, saintly and have everything worked out before they come to God. People tend not to see the mess and muck of their lives as a sacred place, and yet that is the very place where the action happens. "God is closer to us than we are to ourselves," said St. Augustine, a former "wild man," who eventually realized that he had been forgiven. This insight is life changing: that God holds me close, loves me, and desires the best for me. It is a solid foundation that I can build my life on, an anchor in the storms of life, that brings me through even the darkest hours.

These insights are based on the spirituality of St. Ignatius of Loyola, a soldier whose pride was destroyed when he damaged his leg in a 16th-century battle and had to be carried home on a stretcher. Long days of convalescence led to him daydreaming a lot, and he noticed that his moods differed depending on what he thought about. This was a new method of finding God in every aspect of life and in daily reality. It was based on simply reflecting or looking back on personal experience and the careful weighing of decisions to determine how to move forward. As a limping pilgrim, putting his spirituality into practice, he walked the roads of Europe, knowing the extremes of hunger and enduring health problems. He was able to detect the movements of God in his own heart and actions, realizing that God was in continual communication with him, drawing him toward particular actions and outcomes. Using this book, you can uncover this method for yourself and experience these urgings within your own heart.

The photos are designed as visual meditations while the written reflections are based around themes, and the reflection questions are invitations go a bit deeper with the theme. Each theme fits into the process of life, pain, struggle, and growth.

Life

It is characteristic of God and his angels to bring to the soul true happiness and spiritual joy; and to drive from it sadness and trials.

St. Ignatius of Loyola

The
Sacred Heart

The Sacred Heart

The heart is made up of four chambers. The upper two chambers are called atria and the lower two are known as ventricles. On the right side of the heart, the atrium and ventricle work to pump oxygen-poor blood to the lungs. On the left side, the atrium and ventricle combine to pump oxygen-rich blood to the body.

When they combine in perfect harmony, a transaction takes place. That which is lacking arrives in the heart (oxygen-poor blood), it is taken to the lungs and refreshed, and then it is sent back out enriched. How complex, efficient, and amazing is this muscle that lies within each of us.

Take a moment and consider this notion of a transaction taking place. What occurs in the blood within the heart is so similar to what occurs in our lives. Just like blood, we can become in need of being enriched. We can (and do) lose our way in life, become disconnected from healthy ways of living and being with ourselves and others. We can also find ourselves feeling lackluster or even burnt out.

At these times, we need somewhere we can be enriched and renewed. We, just like the blood within us, need to go to the source, be filled again, and then re-enter everyday life. The good news is, of course, that we don't need to go through the incredibly complex and sophisticated processes that our blood does. We don't even have to go very far from where we are.

The key to becoming enriched and refreshed is to connect to the source of all life: the meaning of our existence. We call that God or the loving heart of Jesus, always available to us. Taking some time in prayer, meditation, reflection, reading, or discussion can lead us to the transaction where the tired or lost, the sad or lonely, can become hope-filled once more and ready for the next step in the adventure of life.

Why not take a few minutes right now to relax. Sit quietly, pause, and think about what areas of your life could do with being enriched. Enter a conversation with God, right now. Let the transaction begin. You could see it as a kind of life-blood transfusion. Be open to and curious about what insights might come from this quiet time with God.

The heart holds a wonderful blueprint for the transaction of life itself. Perhaps that is why, in our tradition, we refer to the Sacred Heart of Jesus, the heart burning with love for all; it is beating this very minute with love for you.

Reflection Questions

1. What drains me of life?

– work

– family

– quiet

2. How can I make time for this daily "transfusion" of life?

pray before bed

3. How can I remain connected to the source of life?

worship songs

The Sacred Heart

Individually
Loved

Individually Loved

L ook at this old tree. It is tired. It is covered in vines that make it look untidy and messy. It is not one of the pretty, vibrant-looking trees.

And yet, looking closer, we see that it has an identity badge on it, just like all the trees in this area. It is seen as no different from the others by the one who identified, cares for, and knows the trees.

If this is how it goes for a tree, then how much more so for us?

We may be tired. We may be less vibrant than others. We may be old. We may feel useless. We may be judged by others. We may be getting rough and feel very alone. We may be messy and living messy lives.

But God knows each of us and has marked each of us, *all* of us. Just as the tree curator knows the trees individually, so it is with God.

Let us chew that one over and see where it takes us this new day.

Reflection Questions

1. What is unique about you?

School Spirit spunk

2. What do others see in you that you may not recognize in yourself?

3. What have you to offer to the world?

- cheerfulness
- strength
- friendship

Individually Loved

The Gift
of Time

The Gift of Time

Some thoughts:

* These rocks were formed millions of years ago.
* By the end of this week, we will have taken approximately 161,000 breaths.
* Each of these breaths will involve a process of taking in air, converting it into its constituent parts, using that which we need, and giving away that which we don't. That right there, folks, is the miracle of life.
* Most of us, most of the time, don't even know we're breathing; we simply get on with it.
* Some of us will have birthdays this week.
* Some of us will have hospital appointments this week.
* Sickness will visit someone we know this week.
* For some, their life on this earth will come to an end this week.
* Others will be born into this world.
* It only takes a minute to say a prayer—there will be 10,080 said this week.
* If you dedicated one hour this week to helping someone vulnerable, elderly, lonely, or homeless, you'd still have another 167 hours to play with.

Weeks come and go. As we get older, they seem to go more quickly. It would be easy (and a shame) to forget how much a week can hold. This week will hold a path full of possibilities and experiences. All we have to do is take a step along the path and keep our eyes open along the way.

Reflection Questions

1. Concentrate on your breathing for a moment to see if you are alive!

2. How could I make better use of the time given to me?

3. What are the things that I waste time on, and how could I handle them better?

The Gift of Time

Freedom to Say Yes

Freedom to Say Yes

O ur lives are filled with people who say and who have said yes. They have said yes to doing the right thing. They have said yes to taking on a difficult but worthy path. They have said yes to love and self-sacrifice. They have said yes to God.

Spend a few minutes now and call some of these people to your mind. They might be your parents or grandparents, husband or wife, friend or teacher. It might be a famous person you know about.

Saying yes is a vital part of our relationship with God, as is our freedom to say no as well. I look back now on so many times in my life and see clearly that I said no (even if I didn't understand it as saying no to God at the time). Thank God, I can recall some times of saying yes too. Saying yes to God enables us to be the living presence of love, joy, and mercy in this world. Our yes always draws us to love and value ourselves, others, and the world around us.

In Christian history and tradition, there are numerous people who said yes: Mary, Jeremiah, Moses, and Peter, for example. Their yeses mattered. They may not have known exactly what they were saying yes to, and they certainly didn't know where their yeses would take them (both the pain and the glory). But they had the wisdom to know that God was asking and that they should say yes.

If you're faced with a difficult yes at the minute, remember you're in good company with those above. Know this too: those who say yes are gifted for that yes (so we see Peter, the uneducated fisherman, become a wise man and leader of a new movement—a saint). You too will be gifted for your yes.

Reflection Questions

1. What do you need to say no to?

2. What do you need to be saying yes to?

3. How will you know which response God wants from you?

Freedom to Say Yes

Irrepressible Mystery

Irrepressible Mystery

O ur lives are often shrouded in mystery. Events happen (or don't happen), and we feel confused, bemused, amazed, or anxious. What does it all mean? Is there a purpose to anything at all? We can have so many questions.

Some seek certainty in the face of mystery. We seek it in science. We seek it in rules. We seek it in religion. We seek it in a combination of all these.

And yet, mystery still exists. Just when we feel certain about this or that, something happens to us or to the world around us to cause uncertainty to return and the mystery to continue.

We are faced with illness, grief, natural disaster, terrorism, political upheaval, untimely death, poverty, and cruelty, and we wonder: What is this all about?

Equally we are faced with or experience extreme self-sacrifice, generosity beyond belief, selfless love, wisdom, and leadership, and we wonder: Where did that come from?

Life itself is a mystery. And a glorious one at that! How did we get here? What is life all about? Wonderful mysteries!

Perhaps in the face of these mysteries, we could simply—just for a short while—rest in the mystery.

Just let it be. Let life be what it is. Experience it for the highs and lows it brings.

Don't try to explain it. Don't try to control it. Just *be* in it. Acknowledge that we don't know it all and that we can't know it all.

Resting here, I've a feeling we'll meet with God.

Reflection Questions

1. Where do you experience mystery in your life?

2. How do you deal with mystery (reject, wonder, or examine)?

3. How can you live with mystery as a positive source of life?

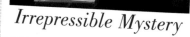

Irrepressible Mystery

Breathe Life

Breathe Life

L et's take a moment, just a short while together, to reflect and to pray. Even if you're not normally a praying person, why not give this a go. It'll do no harm at all, I promise you.

Let's begin by simply breathing. Close your eyes and notice your breath. Don't try to change it at all; just notice it. If you notice it, you're alive! Just dwell on this for a while. Maybe think to yourself, *I am breathing. I am alive. I have life.*

Stay in this moment. If you find yourself wandering or judging yourself or others, just come back to your breath. Feel it go in and out of your body. Your body rises on the in-breath and falls on the out-breath. Feel the movement. And stay with your breath. Do this for a full minute before reading on.

Breathing is one core activity of life. In our breath, so much of the story of life is held. At times, breathing is easy and relaxed. We hardly notice these times. In fact, we take them for granted very often. We know this because at other times our breathing is not so easy.

Take a few minutes now and notice the ebb and flow of your life.

Notice the easy times (here also read joyful times, playful times, peaceful times) and be truly thankful for them. Whatever your concept of God, I invite you, if you wish, to give some thanks to God for these times. God would like that!

Now dedicate some space to the difficult times (here also read sad times, disappointing times, shameful times, angry times). Notice them. Maybe you're in the middle of one right now. Maybe not. See them for what they are: yes, difficult (maybe even awful), but also temporary. All things pass. I invite you to ask God to be with you in these times.

Now return to your breath. Don't try to change it at all; just notice it. Feel it go in and out of your body. Your body rises on the in-breath and falls on the out-breath. Feel the movement. And stay with your breath. With each breath say: "I am breathing. I am alive. I have life."

Reflection Questions

1. What can you do to remember to focus on your breath during difficult times?

2. What are the big ebb-and-flow moments of your life?

3. What can you do to live with change and constant movement?

Breathe Life

Holding On to
the Moment

Holding On to the Moment

You've probably been there. After working for an hour with a friend on an important report, we suddenly realized that before shutting the document down we had forgotten to save it. No! All the marvelous talking, thinking, discerning, and typing we had done—gone! And not coming back. For a moment, we sat in wonderful denial. *No*, we thought, *it's probably there somewhere*. We opened the document, but no. So we closed it. And opened it again, just in case. No, it was gone. Our next reaction was to simply stare at the screen in silence and then look at each other in resignation. We groaned and tried to move on.

Reflecting on this experience, it seems that there can be many lost moments in life, moments that we neglect to save in our memory banks or that we don't recognize at the time as being worthy of saving. Then there are the many moments that pass us by, unsaved, because we are too busy with work or we are too wrapped up in something that, in the moment, feels important but, at a later time, reveals itself as trivial.

The really important stuff could be: moments of relationship and interpersonal contact; simple things like the sunrise and sunset; the smell of the rain; the heat of the (elusive) sun; the quiet whisperings of God in everyday happenings.

Just as the experience on the computer was one of regret and frustration, so it can be with those real-life unsaved moments. Think about those times when we lose people to death or illness. In times of grief, as we hold on to our memories of our lost loved one as being precious, we often wish that we could remember more, call them to mind more, even in the mundane moments of life we shared. Remembering is important.

Slow yourself down and take time to consider the following reflection questions on the next page.

Reflection Questions

1. What happened today that is worth saving?

2. What lessons can I learn from the day?

3. What will I want to remember about this day in five years' time?

Holding On to the Moment

Struggle

Go forth and set the world on fire.
St. Ignatius of Loyola

Endings

Endings

So many times we have faced endings. We think of things in our lives that we were sad to end, but that ending was not a tremendously big deal. Things like hobbies we used to be involved in, jobs we had, courses we attended. The ending of these things is sad in a way, but it is usually easy enough to move on.

Then we think of things that ended but whose ending was a big deal: relationships and friendships mostly. Sometimes, these ended because of our own decisions but often not. The ending may have been out of our control, perhaps a decision by someone else or even a bereavement.

Reflecting on these things that end, we can see that all that is left are lessons learned—love.

So if you're facing endings tonight, here are a few things to bear in mind:

* Even the most difficult feelings of hurt and abandonment ease over time.
* You are a beautiful, cool, good person.
* Everyone makes mistakes and deserves forgiveness.
* Death is not the end; it's a transition.
* You can hold your dead loved ones in your prayers.

- Cherish the love you had.
- You are loved.
- Look back and learn the lesson, then move on in love of others.
- Some endings are good.
- Endings are usually followed by beginnings of something new.
- Reach out to those who love you.
- The dark of night is inevitably followed by the explosive light of a new day. (The ancients thought that in winter the sun died and was reborn in spring).

Reflection Questions

1. Leaving your negativity aside, what are you grateful for?

2. How do you see good working through you?

3. How would you live if you knew you were loved?

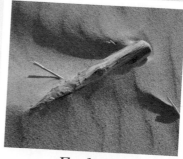

Endings

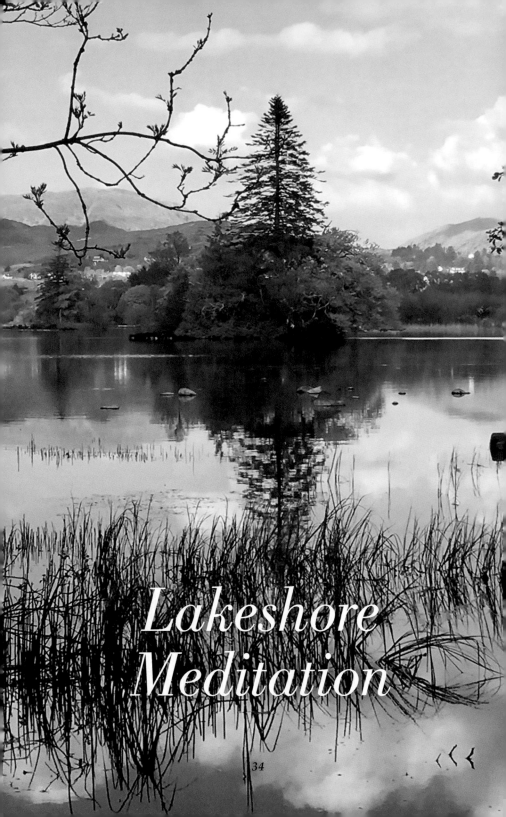

Lakeshore
Meditation

Lakeshore Meditation

ake a few minutes in relaxed meditation.
You might want to read the Gospel of John,
chapter 21, verses 9–14. But you don't need
to do that to enjoy this meditation. Find yourself
a place to sit or lie down. Breathe easily for a few
minutes. Notice the breath go in and go out again.
Feel what it does to your body as your chest and
stomach rise with the breath in and then fall again
with the breath out. Feel your body and its rhythm
as you breathe. As the seconds pass by, you may
feel your body get heavier on the chair or bed. This
is good. This is a sign you are relaxing.

Now use the sight of your mind's eye—your
imagination. Compose a scene. You are by the
shore of a lake at first light. The waters are still and
the shore is rocky. The sky is clear and the morning
sun is shining down. Use your senses to create
this place in your mind. What do you see around
you? What do you hear? What do you smell? By
the shore, there is a small charcoal fire burning.
There is some bread cooking on the fire, as well as
some small fish. Again, use your senses here. See
the flames dance. Hear the fire crackle. Smell the
smoke and the food cooking. Now, see yourself
sitting by the heat of the fire. The fire is warming

you and creating a sense of safety. As you sit here,
Jesus comes and sits beside you. He has cooked the
food and has come to share it with you. What does
his face look like? What does he wear?

Jesus holds you in a loving gaze, the depth and
compassion of which you have never experienced
before. It is clear that you are the apple of his eye.
What do you say to him? What does he say to you?
Spend as much time as you want in the company of
Jesus around this fire, talking and listening. When
you are ready, leave the fire by the lake and focus
once more on your breathing and on your body.
Take three deep and easy breaths. Open your eyes,
refreshed and enlightened by your time with Jesus
and ready to go on with your day.

Reflection Questions

1. What conversation do you need to have with Jesus?

2. What do you need to say to him?

3. What do you need to hear from him?

Lakeshore Meditation

Reflected
Light

Reflected Light

Once a child was heard correcting an adult who said that the moon had been shining brightly the night before. The child listened and then said, "The moon has no light of its own. It shines because it reflects the light of the sun." Brilliant! And true.

We are like the moon. There are days when we have no light of our own. In fact, there are days when we are pretty dark. If we met ourselves on those days, we'd be a bit flat and lackluster.

There are other days when we are like the moon in another way: we have no light of our own, but we do shine a bit. On these days, we reflect others' light back out into the world: the love and friendship and support we get from others. Even though we may be a bit flat or lackluster, on these days we feel lighter; and hopefully others see that in us.

To have others in our lives who give us light is so important. Being connected to them keeps us going. It keeps us focused on the realities of life. It keeps our heads above water on the difficult days.

Pause now and give thanks for the people in your life who give you their light so that you can reflect it back out into the world.

Now, take a minute and think about someone or some people whose lives you might shine a little light into. Remember, others are like the moon too.

The spiritual path in life involves embracing the fact that we are indeed like the moon: we have no light of our own. Any light we have comes from outside us. We believe it comes from God. And we believe that God wants to shine light into all of our lives, for all of us. We have only to be open to letting the light in.

Reflection Questions

1. What is the light I need to live by?

2. How can I be more transparent for reflecting light?

3. Where do I need to let my light shine?

Reflected Light

Let Your Light Shine

Let Your Light Shine

What is our "light"? It could refer to our talents and abilities. It could refer to our ability to love, show mercy, and forgive. What else? Perhaps you could spend a few minutes alone or with a trusted other, considering the ways that you bring your individual form of light to the world.

Light is always contrasted with darkness, the absence of light. There are many forms of darkness in our world today, including depression, loneliness, and despair. These extinguish the light in us, but they are not the whole truth. We are creatures of the light and created out of God's love. Consider the ways that the darkness may get to you, or even convince you that's all there is to life. What do you need to do to live more in the light?

Here are a few suggestions for letting your light shine today:

- Sing a song for someone.
- Hug a friend who is lonely.
- Give some money/coffee/food to a homeless brother or sister.
- Smile at strangers and bid them good day.
- Forgive a wrong.
- Ask for forgiveness from someone you have wronged.

- Make your partner a cup of tea and tell them you love them.
- Pray for peace in the world.
- Go out of your way to do a favor for someone who needs it.

Go shine!

Reflection Questions

1. How is the light within me, and what do I have to do to allow it to grow?

2. How could I radiate more light where I live? What is the darkness I need to resist?

3. What would life be like if I believed that my inner light was transforming me?

Let Your Light Shine

Joy and Happiness

Joy and Happiness

J oy and happiness are two different things, although they are obviously related. There are things in our lives we feel happy doing or experiencing. For example, watching a good movie makes us feel happy for the time we're watching it. Happiness is very much in the moment, and it can be good. But joy is a different thing. Joy is a deeper sense than happiness. We feel happy watching a film but feel joy when we see a good friend we haven't seen for a while. Joy is different.

Having that extra glass of wine, or that bigger slice of cake, might make us happy in the moment, but the next day (or sooner) we may feel that it wasn't such a good idea. Joy is different here too. The things that give us joy do not come with the sense that they might not be a good thing. The things that make us joyful are the things that make us whole, or make us grow, or show us that life is good and precious.

Going swimming or doing other exercise *may* make us feel tremendously happy. But reflecting on the fact that we have the ability and opportunity to do this may fill us with a sense of joy and thankfulness. Thus, we are happy in the moment, joyful after the moment.

Then there are actions that might not make us very happy in the moment but leave us with joy. We think here of making a sacrifice for someone. In the moment, we might feel aggrieved or put out. After the fact, reflecting on the sacrifice we've made, we might feel joy at having done a good thing or the right thing.

To live lives of joy is not to depend on happiness or temporary experiences. It is to seek out the better path and walk it. It is to see the good and the better in all people and to love them. It is to know that we too are loved, held, cherished, and special.

Reflection Questions

1. What makes you happy?

2. What makes you joyful?

3. How can you live more in joy?

Joy and Happiness

Forces
Working
on Us

Forces Working on Us

A s a woman went for a prayer walk and climb one day, she became aware of two opposing forces at work. Firstly, gravity pulled at her (more so as she got higher up). Its force was drawing her downward. She couldn't see it, but—my goodness—could she feel it! The second force at work came from within her. It was the force of muscle, sinew, and tendon. This force kept her moving onward and upward.

She had to work hard to battle the downward force of gravity. It would have been easy to simply give up. But she didn't. And she was rewarded with a great walk and some amazing sights of God's wonderful world all around her.

We all experience the downward drag in life in all sorts of other ways too. Maybe we are suffering anxiety, depression, or worry. Maybe we are experiencing sickness or money worries or relationship difficulties.

That downward drag feels very forceful indeed, but here is a second force at work—a force deep within ourselves. It is a force for good. We believe it to be the presence of the Holy Spirit dwelling within all of us, every single one of us.

Pray that today, no matter what might be dragging you down, you may also experience the power of God's goodness in your life.

Reflection Questions

1. What are the downward pressures in your life?

2. What are the upward pressures in your life?

3. How could you change the balance?

Forces Working on Us

Connected/ Related to Others

Connected/Related
to Others

Aman was in the local shop and, when it came to paying, the shop assistant asked if he wanted to use the contactless function on the debit card machine. This meant that he simply showed his card to the machine, near enough for it to be read and for the money to be taken from his account. No putting the card into the machine, no inputting his pin number, no chance for it to go wrong. Easy! He said goodbye and left.

As he walked from the shop, though, he became uneasy in his spirit. He contemplated that experience over the following days and came to an understanding about why he felt uneasy. It is this: society and technology at times move us to a presumption of no contact with each other—a contactless society, if you will. Lives can be lived ever more remotely, thanks in part to social media and advances in computer technology. Friendships are found, developed, and sometimes ended in virtual reality without the people actually meeting.

We seem to be moving more and more toward a contactless society in which our own existence and our own needs are of primary importance and meeting these needs can be done without contact with another live human being. Not only that, but less contact with others means less insight into the needs of others as well, and in that situation others suffer and we are deprived of the experience of developing empathy and helping our fellow human beings. Our drive toward a contactless society will deprive us of many things, not least the richness that comes from sometimes messy face-to-face contact with another human being.

Reflection Questions

1. How could we create a more-contact society?

2. How could you develop more opportunities to be with, learn from, and help others?

3. How could you help those already in a contactless world and reach out in love to them wherever and whenever possible?

Connected/Related to Others

Pain

Take, Lord, receive all
I have and possess;
give me only your love,
that's enough for me.

St. Ignatius of Loyola

Depression

Depression

There are those among us—our family, friends, colleagues—who are caught up in what seems to be an unending onslaught of problem after problem, heartache after heartache, and grief after grief. These things can lead us to experience depression. Many of us know depression, either as a constant, unwelcome guest or as an intermittent visitor into our lives. Depression can eat away at the core of a person, leaving us lost, all at sea and feeling totally washed up. We feel adrift—cut loose from the things that anchor us to a sense of safety, order, or purpose. Perhaps you are experiencing some of these times yourself at present. If not, I'm sure you know someone who is.

These times can leave us feeling very afraid. We fear to think about what might be coming at us next. We may even cry out, "Give me a break! Enough already." Another feeling that comes at these times is a feeling of not being loved or cared for. We may feel very alone or angry at ourselves, others, the world, and God.

In this ocean of despair, we can be tempted to just give up. But don't. Wait. There's another story going on here.

In these times of despair, when we're all at sea, there are people who care. There are people who love us. And God loves us especially in these moments. Reaching out for help can be a really tough thing to do but is always a good thing to do. So is checking in with those we feel might be suffering from depression. We can be a listening ear or simply a positive presence in what can seem like a totally negative situation.

Reflection Questions

1. How do I experience depression?

2. What helps me get through it?

3. What help do I need to ask for?

Depression

Surviving
Suffering

Surviving Suffering

T his journey of life is filled with such beauty at times. We could all do with slowing down and appreciating that beauty more often. Too often, we allow it to pass us by without recognition.

We do sometimes catch it, though. Sometimes, we realize we are in the presence of beauty, and we allow ourselves to freeze time—to stay in that presence. In those moments, we are conscious enough to really experience beauty. While these moments may not come very often, when they do, they are often very emotional.

They connect us to a central truth that no matter what suffering there is in the world (and there is suffering in this world) and in our lives (there is and will be suffering in our lives), there is also beauty. We cannot explain why it is so; we can only accept that it is so.

This acceptance thing is hard to do. However, in accepting suffering, we are also free to accept, and savor all the more, the beauty we see and experience in the world.

Try praying for others: hold close to your heart in prayer all those who are suffering at this time; hold close to your heart in prayer all those who are sick; hold close to your heart in prayer all those who do not or cannot see beauty in their lives at this moment.

Reflection Questions

1. What is the beauty now in my life?

2. What is the suffering in my life?

3. What can I do to see the beauty beyond suffering?

Surviving Suffering

Converting
Violence

Converting Violence

Isn't wood really lovely? In particular, tone wood—that is, wood that is believed to possess qualities that make it resonate in such a way that it produces beautiful sounds. These woods are used in the production of musical instruments, such as guitars. Not only do these woods sound beautiful, they often look beautiful when treated well. The beauty is in the uncovering of the grain within the wood, revealed when the outer covering is stripped away and when we see the heart of the wood for what it is, in all its splendor.

The tone of these woods is heard when the wood is made to vibrate in some way. With guitars, this happens when you strike the string or strike the wood itself. In one way, this is a kind of violent action. Even striking softly is striking. What the wood does with this violence is to convert it into beauty. What a way to subvert and convert violence, to turn it into something beautiful. Jesus was the ultimate example of the violence of the world being radically turned into beauty and peace—and redemption and salvation to boot!

We've seen examples of this kind of subversion and conversion in humans too. Gandhi and Martin Luther King embodied a kind of radical pacifism. The former was inspired by Hinduism, the latter by Christianity; both were inspired by the violent suffering of their people. These, and others, have become beautiful "tone wood" for the world to hear. The tone of their words and wisdom resonates and resounds throughout history as a constant call to peaceful living, even or maybe particularly in the face of violence. The tune they play can often strike an unharmonious chord with our own less-than-peaceful actions. At these times, we are challenged to tune ourselves again and to live in harmony with those around us.

We are often visited by violence in our lives. For some, this violence is on a small scale. For others among us, it is violence on a bigger scale. We don't have to look too far to see this violence: Syria, Palestine, Ankara, Belgium, Paris, South Sudan, and in our own cities.

Reflection Questions

1. How do I react to violence? Can I subvert or transform it?

2. Where is there violence in my life or environment?

3. How do I choose to face violence? Whom do I follow who inspires me?

Converting Violence

Woundedness

Woundedness

Wounds are important sources of our life stories.

The journey through life is one that inevitably involves a certain wounding of us all. Sometimes this is a physical wounding. And sometimes it is an emotional or spiritual wounding. Either way, being wounded seems to be part of the deal for us all.

And being wounded is not pleasant. In fact, sometimes it's downright awful. We can feel like we will never recover at all from our wounding.

Yet wounds can heal. It may take time and lots of help or support. But they can heal—and when they do, they provide us with a different perspective on life.

Some years ago, a friend had a bad cartilage tear in his right knee that necessitated surgery. He spent eight months on crutches and painkillers before the surgery. It was not a great time. However, he had surgery, and eventually the wounds healed. This time of woundedness left him with a renewed sense of how much of a gift life can be. Just for him to walk unaided, albeit for fewer miles than before, was marvelous!

Death and bereavement wound also. Even years after a bereavement, the wound can still feel raw and open. This loss (and others) can also leave us with a real sense of the importance of life, friendship, and the love of God.

When we expose our woundedness to others, it invites them into the story of our wounds. It is often more difficult to be judgmental, angry, or prejudicial with someone when we appreciate their woundedness.

Maybe that's why God allowed Jesus to be so horribly wounded: to let us know the value of wounds. And why Thomas had to see Jesus' wounds to truly believe in his Resurrection.

Reflection Questions

1. Can you be grateful for healed wounds? If not, how can you seek it?

2. Ask for healing for those wounds that need it.

3. With whom can you trust that your woundedness will be respectfully received?

Woundedness

Fear

Fear

Many of us live with, or even in, fear part of the time.

We often fear things we don't know yet. Will I lose my job in these austere times? Will my relationship end? Will I be judged by others? Will I fail at the things I'm trying to achieve?

This type of fear limits us in so many ways. We can almost become the things we fear most by fearing them in the first place. We do not quite know how this happens, but it seems to be so.

Living in fear is like living in a box. The space we inhabit is small. Our journeys in life are short and mainly unsatisfactory. Life becomes claustrophobic and a chore.

Only when we break free from fear can we see how big and full of possibilities life actually is. And once we see this, we're less likely to fall back into fear. The trick is breaking free for the first time.

It's no coincidence, therefore, that the most common thing Jesus and other major spiritual teachers tell us is "be not afraid." It seems to have been the cornerstone of what he taught us—the only way to begin a truly enlightened spiritual path.

Instead of fearing, we can simply trust. Trust that things will be OK even in the midst of the pain and misery that come our way. Things will be OK, because there is a bigger story, a bigger picture, a better picture, a story with a great ending. From a Christian perspective, we trust that God is working with us, in us, and through us.

We can't make ourselves *not* be afraid. But we can develop the ability to trust and see the big picture. This will happen mostly through silence, centering ourselves, and praying. It will also happen if we read, listen to, and hang out with people who are not afraid. Find these books and these people and keep them close.

Reflection Questions

1. In what ways can you acknowledge your need of One who is bigger than yourself?

2. How can you move beyond fear and into trust, consciously shifting your focus?

3. Who are the wise teachers and friends who could accompany you on this journey?

Fear

Dark Night

Dark Night

Darkness has long been associated with negativity. We are said to be in a dark mood when we feel low. We are said to be kept in the dark when someone is purposely not telling us the full facts of situations that we face. In this part of the world, we often speak with a sense of dread about the dark afternoons and evenings of winter. Everything seems dead, and nothing grows. And there's something not quite exhilarating about getting up for work in the dark!

There are so many people feeling like we're in dark times. Today alone, I heard about frustrations at work, job loss, family disputes, illness, worry, and more. Let's spend a moment now and call to our minds those we know who are in dark times right now. Unite yourself with them and their suffering.

The antidote to darkness is light, as we know. During spring, we really begin to see the evenings get longer. In fact, from then on, people will be going to and coming from work in the light. Wonderful! The journey seems easier on these days. In winter, it seems that the darkness of the journey is total and complete. And yet spring is just around the corner.

The lesson of this world around us is that light will replace darkness.

Let's take a moment and pray (if it's your thing) for those in dark times right now (or maybe spare a thought or hold them in your heart if praying isn't your thing) that they too will come out of these dark times and into lighter times.

Jesus is known as many things. One name that he called himself was the Light of the World. Let us pray that his light shines on us all these days.

Reflection Questions

1. What/who is the light of your life?

2. What is the darkness you experience?

3. How can you live in the light?

Dark Night

Dealing with Anger

Dealing with Anger

A therapist was working with a young person who had great difficulty with anger. It had got her in trouble with her family, friends, school, and even the police. In fact, she found it hard to talk about her anger—it made her angry. So, one day, the therapist asked her to draw her anger instead of talk about it. She agreed, and when she had finished she had drawn her anger as a red-hot ember. It was black and foreboding at its base but deep, deep red from there on up. Without saying a word, she had told the therapist how she felt inside.

If any of us were to hold a red-hot ember in our hand, we would want to get rid of it as soon as possible; we wouldn't want to hold on to it. If we did, we would suffer! And in getting rid of it, we would probably try to be as careful as we could not to set fire to things or people around us. We would get rid of it in as safe and manageable a way as we possibly could.

The problem is that we often hold on to anger. In fact, we often allow that anger to turn inward, to the point that we can be angry with others and ourselves at the same time! We can hold on to that red-hot ember of anger and allow it to burn away at us. This is not such a good idea. We are not free to discern what God is calling us to if we cannot see beyond the red-hot embers.

And then there is the anger that goes out from us. Do we dispose of that particular red-hot ember in a safe and manageable way? Sometimes, we do. We find ways of calmly discussing our anger with others or using art, music, or sports. Other times, if we're honest, we don't do so well. We let that red-hot ember loose, and others get burned.

Jesus said, "Anyone who is angry at his brother should go and be reconciled." We are called, therefore, to recognize when we are angry and to seek reconciliation with whomever we are angry with—others or ourselves. This will involve getting to know the movement of our feelings within us. Why not commit tonight to taking a little time each day to recognize the red-hot embers you are holding on to and exploring ways to let them go in a safe and manageable way.

Reflection Questions

1. How do you deal with anger?

2. What are the red-hot embers in your life?

3. How could you deal better with anger?

Dealing with Anger

Moving On from Sorrow

Moving On from Sorrow

F ind a place to sit or lie down where you can be silent and undisturbed for a few minutes. Breathe and notice the breath go in and go out again. Feel what it does to your body as your chest rises with the breath in and then falls with the breath out. Feel your body and its rhythm as you breathe. As the seconds pass by, you may feel your body get heavier on the chair or bed. This is good. This is a sign that you are relaxing. Stay with the sensation of your chest rising and falling. Allow your mind to settle on this sensation and this part of your body. Inside your chest is your heart. As you breathe, try to tune in to the beats of your heart. You may feel it as a kind of thump or pulse. As you begin to feel it, know that this is a sure sign of life within you.

Now imagine that your heart is a room. See that room inside you. Compose it; create the image of it in your mind's eye. Make it the most comfortable room possible. Use your eyes: what is in the room? Is there furniture? What color are the walls? What covers the floor? Carpet? Tiles? Wood? Something else? Use your ears: what noise, if any, is in this room? Use your nose: what scents fill the room? Remember, this is your room. It can be whatever you want it to be. Now place yourself in the room. See yourself there. Experience yourself there. Are you sitting? Are you standing? Are you lying down? Allow yourself to feel safe, relaxed, and comfortable. In your mind's eye, see Jesus join you in the room. Spend some time now creating this scene. What does he look like? How is his hair? How is his face? How are his eyes? What is his expression? What does he wear? See him there and be wordlessly in his presence. Stay like this for as long as you want.

After a while, bring to Jesus anything in your life that you would like to see transfigured. Is there something that is troubling you? Tell him. Is there someone you know who is suffering? Tell him. Are you in despair? Tell him. Describe to Jesus those areas of your life that are in need of transfiguration. Now, be in his presence again. Know that he will bring all the trouble to an end. Know that he will bring beauty where there is ugliness. Know that he will bring peace where there is conflict. Know that he will bring consolation where there is desolation. Listen to what he says. Be aware of how he looks at you with utter, unconditional love. Note what he teaches you. When you are ready, focus again on your breath and the movement in your chest. Take three deep breaths and leave this meditation with what you heard and saw in the room of your heart.

Reflection Questions

1. What needs to be transformed in you?

2. In what personal dark places are you willing to allow Jesus?

3. How can you bring this transformation to others?

Moving On from Sorrow

Growth

*For it is not knowing much, but
realizing and relishing things
interiorly, that contents and
satisfies the soul.*

St. Ignatius of Loyola

Accepting Myself

Accepting Myself

So many people look in the mirror and don't see what is truly there. They don't see their beautiful, pure essence. Led by the teachings of a world obsessed with its own version of what is acceptable or unacceptable, what is attractive or unattractive they come to hate the image they see. This, in turn, pervades their thinking and can lead to depression and low self-esteem.

This false ideal is created by a media machine concerned more about superficial image than inner worth, and above all concerned with making profits from our efforts to conform to their norm.

If you know someone or if you are someone caught in this trap of non-self-acceptance, then you are part of a large group of people in this society. And it might be good for you to read some things tonight: "You are beautiful, made in the image of God." There are things about your physical looks that, even if you cannot see them, someone finds cute! Your soul and spirit will last longer than the most beautiful person's good looks. The meaning of your existence does not hinge on the flatness of your stomach or the flabbiness of your arms!

All the skinniness in the world does not surpass the doing of loving deeds for another. Your muscles do not need to increase as much as your kindness. You were made this way—it's OK.

Healthy living is a great thing. A healthy body is just as great. Trying to keep in good shape is an honorable pursuit, but only if it is healthy in a physical and emotional sense. And it is best when we are also in good spiritual shape.

Self-acceptance and thanks to the one who made us? Now that is where it's at!

Reflection Questions

1. What positive phrase can you repeat to yourself (a mantra)?

2. From whom can you ask for help with what really bothers you?

3. Imagine how God sees you right now.

Accepting Myself

Believe in the Unseen

Believe in the Unseen

I believe in the existence of the wind. Do you? I have never seen the wind. Have you? And yet I believe the wind exists. Not only that, I believe that the wind is an awesome thing.

Why should this be? I know that some very weighty and academic studies and explanations of the wind have probably been written through the ages. But none of these are the reason I believe that the wind exists. The only reason I believe the wind exists is that I have experienced the wind and its effects. Simple. Full stop. I have experienced it.

I have stood on top of a mountain and felt my body fight with gravity as the wind nearly lifted me up. I have felt the rain hit my face so hard that it hurt me, because the wind blew it so hard. I have heard the roof tiles on my house groan as the wind pulled at them.

It was my experience of the wind that taught me to believe that the wind exists. Books, research, and the word of other people all help verify my belief. But at its core it is down to a personal experience.

I believe in God for the very same reason: I have had a personal experience of God. I have had this experience of God in so many ways in my life: in the love of my family and friends, in the stillness of my prayer life and the sacraments, in the wonderful world of nature.

But in the absence of a personal experience of God, these are only words, books, and rules. They will not live. What will live in the lives of people are experiences. God is made present in the world in many ways. St. Teresa of Avila says that "Christ has no body now but yours." This means that we are often called to be the presence (experience and effect) of God in the world.

Reflection Questions

1. Where do you experience God personally in your life?

2. What difference does/would such an experience make to your life?

3. How would you act differently in light of this?

Believe in the Unseen

The Web
of Life

The Web of Life

T his picture makes no sense at all. The weight of the water molecules gathered along the threads of the web far outweigh the web itself. Therefore, it would make more sense if the web folded under the pressure, and yet it does not. It stays strong under the pressure and holds together. No sense at all.

Why does this happen? It seems that there is something about the silk that the web is composed of—it is made of strong stuff. There are many connections between the threads, strengthening the structure. The spider is the source of the silk and builder of the web. Put these ingredients together and it now makes sense.

Our lives are like this web at times. We can become sodden, weighed down by troubles. Look at the threads of the web in the picture. It is clear that there are many, many droplets of water hanging on each thread, like so many small and big worries, anxieties, and problems that we face. And yet we too are made of strong stuff. Take a moment and call to mind all the difficult situations you have faced in your life to date. You have made it this far. You have coped with and overcome a lot. Strong stuff indeed.

And then there is the source of life—we call that source God. We believe that God gave life to each one of us. We believe God wants us to spin a beautiful interconnected web through life, strengthening each other as we go. And we believe that God, the source, can give us strength as we face the heaviness of life's worries and problems. How do we connect to the source?

We can do so through prayer, silence, reflection, music, nature, art, liturgy, service, love, and mercy, to name but a few. These are the true threads of the web of a well-lived, beautiful life.

Reflection Questions

1. What are the important connections in your life, the "threads" that support you?

2. What are the things that weigh you down, that feel overpowering?

3. What is the source of your inner strength, the unbreakable center?

The Web of Life

Rewind
the Day

Rewind the Day

Take a moment of quiet and reflection. Spend a full minute (or more if you like) simply breathing and focusing on your breath. Notice the breath go in and go out. Feel your body rise with the in-breath and fall with the out-breath. Really notice this. Perhaps you feel your clothes shift a bit as your body moves. If so, really feel this. Notice the coldness of the air as it goes in. And then the warmth as it goes out. Immerse yourself in this experience of breathing for a minute before you read on.

Quietly retrace your day in your mind's eye. Begin with the moment you awoke this morning, right to this very moment. See the events and the people you came across today. Remember the emotions you felt.

Perhaps tune in to the pressure points of the day—those moments of stress or worry or anger or disappointment. Spend a moment with them. Try to see the learning that came here, too. If you're a praying person, you could ask God to be with you in these pressure-point moments.

Now tune in to the moments of happiness, solution, resolution, joy, mercy, love. Spend a few moments reliving these moments. Don't let yourself off the hook by telling yourself there were none of these moments. Maybe they were few and far between, and maybe they were short, but they happened today sometime. Stretch yourself. Savor them. If you're a praying person, you could thank God for these life-giving moments.

Return to your breath again. Feel it go in and go out. As you settle on your breath, I invite you to say a short prayer.

Reflection Questions

1. Do you notice anything significant about your day as you look over it? What is it?

2. Which difficult moments does this pause of reflection help you understand?

3. Do you have any clarity about what you might do tomorrow? If so, what is it?

Rewind the Day

Handling
Distractions

Handling Distractions

Aman took a morning prayer walk today, out into the wilderness (where the best prayer time is to be found). As he walked and prayed, he got into a lovely rhythm. He felt himself calm, relaxed, and at one in prayer.

However, as he walked on into the countryside, the road surface changed. It became smooth and a bit slippery. After a while, his shoes began to make a squeaky noise on the road. Each step was accompanied by an annoying squeak. This sound, out there in the wilderness, with its relative silence broken only by sounds of animals and far-off voices every now and then, seemed discordant. It began to throw him off his rhythm. He found that he wasn't contemplating his prayer intentions as before. He kept getting drawn back to that noise!

Then, he remembered that it was soon to be the feast day of St. Ignatius of Loyola, who had taught his followers to find God in all things.

So, the man thought to himself, *if God is in all things, then God is also in this noise.* Acknowledging that allowed him to pray in a different way. It led him to contemplate the many discordant events we see or experience in our lives. He stayed with the noise of his shoes and brought to mind (and prayer) some of the discordant noises in life. In doing so, he brought the following to his prayer: The bombing and suffering of men, women, and children in so many war-torn places. The prejudice suffered by LGBTQ people around the world. The plight of the poor and homeless all around us. The sick, suffering, and dying. His prayer walk felt very rich this morning. And it was because of St. Ignatius's teaching of finding God in everything—even squeaky noises on a lonely country road.

Reflection Questions

1. What are the annoyances in your life?

2. How could you see them differently?

3. What have you to learn from them?

Handling Distractions

From Small Seeds

From Small Seeds

One of the frustrations we face is when we want to see something change or develop and we want to see it do so in big ways but it does not. We want to see arguments resolved immediately. We want confusion to suddenly lift and clarity to descend like a dove from above! We want to see sadness, anger, and bitterness suddenly dissipate. However, more often than not, things do not change like this. Rather, they change only in small, sometimes almost imperceptible ways. And when it happens like this, we can miss these small moments of change altogether. We simply do not see them. And we can tell ourselves the story that "nothing ever changes" or "things will always be like this." We notice it especially with growing children. On a day-to-day basis, it seems that they are just the same as the last day, but when we step back and take stock, we see that they have grown up before our eyes, almost without us knowing it!

I call these little, almost imperceptible changes "mustard-seed moments" (for those of you who are interested, Jesus talked about mustard seeds. You can find an example in *Mk. 4:30–32*). There are moments in all our lives that, though small, are only parts of an ultimate change that is huge. The cumulative effect of these mustard-seed moments can change our lives—our world, even.

Take, for example, small steps toward peace and reconciliation. Every day, in our world, people are taking brave and selfless steps toward peace and reconciliation by reaching out to traditional enemies or by taking a risk to visit an area or place that would have been off-limits before or by swallowing pride and healing broken relationships. These mustard-seed moments could go by unnoticed. Their cumulative effect, however, could not. Their cumulative effect sets the world alight with peace and love!

Reflection Questions

1. What "mustard-seed moments" are in your life presently?

2. But remember, mustard can burn when we eat it. Are you prepared for the fact that making mustard-seed moments might come at some personal cost and even some discomfort?

3. What can you do to wait with patience for events to play themselves out?

From Small Seeds

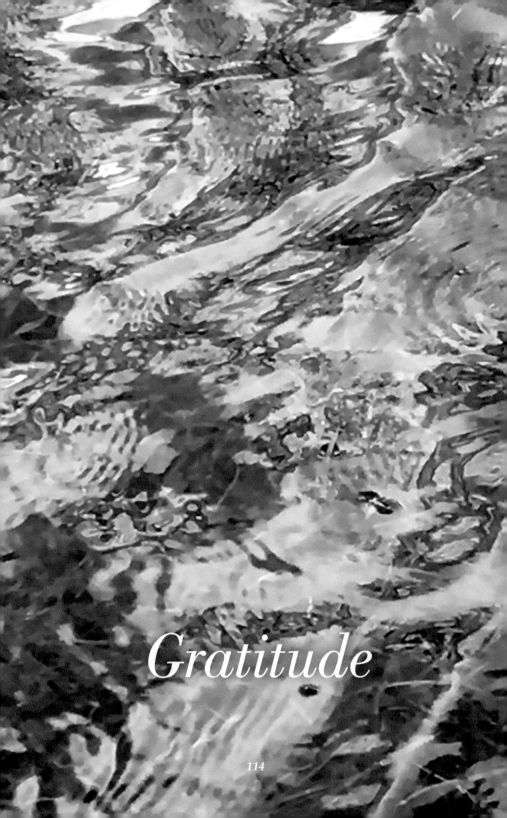

Gratitude

Gratitude

F irst, find a place where you can be still, right where you are now, even if you feel troubled or agitated. Remember that the bottom of a well is always still even if the surface is choppy. Try to make the downward move. In that place, just breathe.

On your in-breath, be thankful that you are alive. You might even say, "Thank you for my life."

On your out-breath, be more aware of living life to the fullest. You might even say, "Help me to live my life to the fullest."

You could repeat this breathing and meditating for as long as you want. As you do, be aware of what comes to your mind and heart.

There might be some insights into how your life is gifted and blessed by the presence of good people or good situations right now. These little gems of gratitude might exist even in the midst of troubles or illness or worries. If we look, they will be there.

There might be some ideas about where God's spirit is moving you to develop in your life.

On the out-breath, become aware of a call from deep within you, drawing you to slow down and to quiet yourself. You may believe this is the Holy

Spirit at work, but you don't have to. Become aware of a drive for constant doing and how it is in conflict with your being. Hear a call to re-evaluate and truly listen to God's call to you.

Reflection Questions

1. What happened for you in this breathing prayer today?

2. How can you more easily reach the deeper part of yourself?

3. How can you live more in this place of calm?

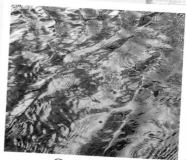

Gratitude

Epilogue

We invite you to close your eyes. As you do, imagine you are standing in a forest. In your mind's eye, look around you. See the shape of the trees rising up from the ground. See the colors of the trunks, the branches, and the leaves. Look at the ground and see what is covering it. Are there leaves, pine needles, or twigs? Now use your imagination to smell the scents of the forest. Perhaps you smell a perfume from the trees or from flowers in the ground around you. In your imagination, what do you hear in the forest? Is it quiet, or is it a noisy forest?

Doing such an exercise can enable you to have a good sense of what a forest is. But the exercise would be complete only if you were able to be in the forest, to take a step from your mind's eye into the real world of everyday experience.

And so the book is at an end. Your eyes have taken in a lot by this stage, either bit by bit through the weeks and months that you spent reading the book, or all at one go if you were especially keen! We hope it has been a rich experience for you.

This book has been partly a reflective prayer tool and partly a road map for negotiating our way through the wonderful messiness of life. Our encouragement as we come to a close is for you to take what you have seen and learned out into the forest of your life's experience. Perhaps you could return to these pages every now and then, taking a break from the journey, to delve deeper into the words and images once more, bringing your experiences to them and seeing what new insights emerge.

Just as God was in the words and images of these pages, so is God in the messiness of everyday life, just waiting for you to encounter him and yearning to hold you in his loving arms. Go meet with him. It will be a great adventure.